The Big Ideas Club Presents

Young Minds

Living Philosophy

Plato's Republic for Kids

The Cave and the Climb

Power, Truth, and the Fate of the City

(Book V-X)

By Jason Kassel, PhD

© 2025

Recursive Publishing

Plato's Garden

Long ago, in the sunlit land of Greece, a man named Plato wrote a strange and beautiful book. It was not a story, but it was full of characters. It was not a poem, but every line reached for something beyond the words. It was called the *Republic*—and it asked one daring question:

What is justice?

But instead of giving an answer, Plato gave us a garden of ideas. In it, people walked and argued. They questioned each other. They told stories. They built imaginary cities. They lit fires in the mind.

At the center stood a man named Socrates—a teacher who didn't give lectures, but asked questions that made people think harder, feel deeper, and see the world differently.

This series invites you to walk in that same garden.

You'll meet Socrates again, but this time, he's joined by a few curious children who ask their own questions and push the conversation forward. Together, they explore one of history's greatest books—not by summarizing it, but by living it: as dialogue, as discovery, as a kind of soul-training.

What You'll Find in These Books

- Dramatic Conversations
  Each chapter presents a faithful, scene-based retelling of Plato's *Republic*, using child-accessible language without losing philosophical depth.

- Under the Olive Tree
  After every chapter, Socrates sits with the children to reflect on the images and words just spoken—inviting the reader into deeper thinking.

- Moral Conversation Prompts
  At the end of each chapter, you'll find thoughtful questions meant for real conversations—at the dinner table, in the classroom, or under your own olive tree.

- A City and a Soul
  As the books unfold, an imaginary city is built. But something else is revealed: that the city is a mirror of your own soul—and that justice begins within.

Why Begin with a City?

Our souls are quiet and hidden. They are hard to see. But a city is large, noisy, clear. Plato believed that by building an imaginary city from the ground up, we could learn to recognize the structure of justice—not just around us, but inside us.

That's why these books are called *The Children of the Chair*. The philosopher's chair—once thought to be for kings—is now offered to anyone who dares to ask: *What kind of life should I live?*

A Note to Grown-Ups

These books do not simplify Plato. They translate him—faithfully, imaginatively, and in conversation with children. Every dialogue, metaphor, and idea comes from the original Greek text, shaped into a form meant to be read aloud, questioned deeply, and remembered for years to come.

The Philosopher Queen

1: Breaking the Rules of the World

(Based on Republic 449a–457b – The equality of women and the role of nature)

Scene:
Socrates stands before a map of the city, drawn on a scroll. The children gather around, Glaucon watching from the side.

Socrates:
Now that our city is well built... who should rule it?

Milo:
The best guardians?

Tessa:
The ones with the strongest souls?

Socrates:
Yes. But now, let me ask a question that may sound strange:
Should women be rulers, too?

Glaucon (laughing):
What? Women? As guardians?

Tessa (quietly):
Why not?

Socrates:
Tell me this—does the soul have a gender?

Milo:
No... it's invisible.

Socrates:
And is the work of ruling done by hands—or by wisdom?

Tessa:
Wisdom.

Socrates:
Then if a woman has a soul that loves truth, learns deeply, and lives justly—why should she be kept from the ruler's chair?

Glaucon:
But won't people laugh?

Socrates (smiling):
Let them laugh. Truth does not bend for laughter.

Under the Olive Tree

(The children sit beneath the olive branches. Glaucon tosses pebbles into a bowl. Tessa frowns, thinking.)

Tessa:
Socrates... why didn't you just say this at the start?

Socrates:
Because the city had to be built first—so we could see who belonged at its top.

Milo:
But people won't accept it easily.

Socrates:
The highest truths often come last—and cost the most to say.

Moral Conversation Prompt:

- Can tradition be wrong—even if everyone believes it?

- What makes someone worthy of leadership?

- Should we ignore laughter when we're standing for truth?

2: The Ruler Who Loves Truth

(Based on Republic 474b–480a – What makes a philosopher fit to rule)

Scene:
Socrates and the children walk along a narrow garden path. A quiet stream trickles nearby. Tessa holds a feather; Milo skips stones. Socrates stops near a tall olive tree.

Socrates:
Now let me ask you something else—harder still. What kind of person should rule?

Milo:
Someone smart.

Tessa:
Someone fair.

Socrates:
Yes. But above all—someone who loves truth.

Tessa:
What do you mean "loves" truth?

Socrates:
Not just knows facts. Not just repeats what's popular.
A philosopher is someone who chases truth the way others chase gold or fame.

Milo:
But... wouldn't they be weird?

Socrates:
They might seem strange—gentle, quiet, slow to speak.
But inside? Their soul burns bright.

Tessa:
What makes them different?

Socrates:
They're not pulled by desire. Not puffed up by praise.
They are steady, like stars. They love learning more than winning.

Milo:
So philosophers aren't just thinkers... they're lovers?

Socrates:
Yes. Lovers of wisdom. That's what the word means.

Under the Olive Tree

(The breeze grows cooler. Socrates leans against the olive tree. Milo balances the feather on his nose.)

Milo:
Socrates, do you think we could become philosophers?

Socrates (smiling):
You already are—if you keep loving questions more than answers.

Tessa:
But if philosophers are so rare... how do we find one to rule?

Socrates:
We train them. Watch them. Wait for them to rise.

Milo:
Even if they don't want power?

Socrates:
Especially then.

Moral Conversation Prompt:

- What does it mean to "love truth"?

- Can someone be wise without being loud or famous?

- Should the best leaders want power—or avoid it?

3: The Storm Against the Wise

(Based on Republic 487b–497a – Why philosophers are mocked, and why the city must protect them)

Scene:
Rain begins to patter on the garden leaves. The children run to a stone shelter with Socrates.
Thunder rumbles. Glaucon enters, shaking his head.

Glaucon:
It's just like what you said, Socrates. People don't trust philosophers.

Tessa:
Why not?

Socrates:
Because true philosophers seem strange to the world.

Milo:
Strange how?

Socrates:
 They speak slowly when others shout.
 They doubt what others cheer.
 They care more about truth than trophies.

Glaucon:
 So people laugh at them?

Socrates:
 Or worse. They call them useless—or dangerous.
 They confuse the real lover of wisdom with the ones
who just pretend.

Tessa:
 Like fake philosophers?

Socrates:
 Yes. Some use big words to look wise.
 But the true philosopher? They seek light—no
matter the cost.

Milo:
 And the city needs that?

Socrates:
 A city without philosophers is like a ship with no
stars.
 It may move fast—but it forgets where it's going.

Under the Olive Tree

(The rain slows. The children huddle under a wide
branch. Socrates draws a tiny ship in the mud.)

Tessa:
If philosophers are so good, why don't people
protect them?

Socrates:
Because storms are loud. Wisdom is quiet.
And the world often follows noise before truth.

Milo:
So... the city must build shelter for its wise?

Socrates:
Yes. Wisdom must be guarded—like fire in the wind.

Tessa:
Even if no one understands it?

Socrates:
Especially then.

Moral Conversation Prompt:

- Have you ever seen someone mocked for being
  thoughtful?

- What's the difference between someone who
  seems wise and someone who truly loves
  wisdom?

- How can a city—or a family—protect its
  thinkers?

4: The Form of the Good

(Based on Republic 504d–509c – The highest idea: the Good itself)

Scene:
 The storm has passed. Golden light breaks through the clouds. Socrates walks with the children toward a hilltop. At the top is a round stone bench, warmed by the sun.

Socrates:
 Now we've asked who should rule. We've said: the one who loves truth.

But here is the next question:
 What is truth made of?

Tessa:
 Isn't truth... facts?

Milo:
 Or things that are real?

Socrates:
 Truth is more than facts.
 Just as the sun is more than light—it gives life.

Tessa:
 So what is the "sun" of the soul?

Socrates:
 I call it... the Form of the Good.

Milo:
That sounds mysterious.

Socrates:
It is. Just as the eye cannot see without the sun, the soul cannot understand without the Good.
It is what all knowledge reaches toward—like flowers to sunlight.

Tessa:
Can we ever see it?

Socrates:
Not with the eyes. But with the soul trained in truth, beauty, and reason.
The Good is not a thing. It is the reason why anything makes sense at all.

Under the Olive Tree

(The sun shines fully now. The children and Socrates sit at the hill's crest. Below, the city spreads like a map.)

Milo:
So "the Good" is like the sun... but inside our minds?

Socrates:
Yes. And just as the sun lets you see the world, the Good lets you understand it.

Tessa:
Why don't people talk about it more?

Socrates:
Because it hides behind simpler things—like rules or rewards.
But the philosopher must go higher. Past opinion. Past fear. To truth.

Milo:
Even if no one else comes?

Socrates:
The one who sees the Good must return—and help others rise.

Moral Conversation Prompt:

- What do you think "the Good" is?

- Can something be good, even if it's not easy or fun?

- Why might people ignore the deepest truths?

5: Returning to the Cave

(Based on Republic 519c–521c – The duty of the philosopher to return and serve)

Scene:
Night falls slowly over the city. Lanterns flicker. Socrates and the children return from the hilltop,

walking in silence. Then Socrates stops before a dark opening in the ground—a cave.

Socrates:
 Let me tell you a story.

Tessa:
 Another one?

Milo:
 Is this about the Good?

Socrates (nodding):
 Imagine a group of people, born inside a cave.
They've been there since childhood—legs and necks in chains.
 They can only see the wall in front of them.

Behind them is a fire. And behind the fire, people hold up shapes—cutouts of trees, animals, people.

The chained ones see only shadows. They think that's the world.

Tessa (eyes wide):
 They don't know they're in a cave?

Socrates:
 No. Now imagine one person is freed. He turns around. At first, the fire hurts his eyes. Then he climbs out. Slowly, painfully, he sees the real world— trees, stars, the sun.

And then... he goes back.

Milo:
 Back into the cave?

Socrates:
 Yes. To tell the others.
 But they don't believe him. They say the journey
made him blind. They threaten him.

Tessa:
 But he saw the truth.

Socrates:
 And that is the fate of the philosopher.
 To rise toward the Good—and return for those still
in the dark.

Under the Olive Tree

(The cave opening fades in the darkness. The
children sit beside Socrates. The stars glow above.)

Milo:
 Why return? Why not stay in the light?

Socrates:
 Because wisdom is not a prize to keep. It's a gift to
share.

Tessa:
 Even if no one listens?

Socrates:
 Even then. Especially then.

Milo:
So the philosopher's reward is... duty?

Socrates:
Yes. To see—and to serve. That is the path of the philosopher-ruler.

Moral Conversation Prompt:

- If you discovered something true—but no one believed you—would you still speak?

- Why is it hard to leave comfort and return to challenge?

- How can we bring light to dark places?

Conclusion: The Philosopher Queen

This chapter dared to ask questions that many people—even today—find strange:

Can women rule?
Can truth be loved more than fame?
Can a wise person lead without wanting power?

Socrates showed the children that justice is not about keeping old customs—but about seeking what is good, even when it costs. In the just city, wisdom sits on the throne. Philosophy is not just thinking—it is a kind of love. And those who love truth the most are the ones most fit to lead.

But the world often laughs at the wise. And the path to truth can be hard, lonely, and full of storms. That's why the philosopher must be brave—not just with words, but with the soul.

And when the philosopher climbs out of the shadows and sees the Good... their duty is not done.

They must return.

Back into the cave.
 Back into the noise.
 Back to help the others rise.

This is the great calling of the just soul—not to rule over, but to serve alongside.

And now, the children understand:
 The real throne is not gold or silver. It is a quiet seat—in the mind, in the soul, in the garden of questions.

 Final Section

 Try It Yourself: Truth-Seeker's Challenge

Find one rule, habit, or tradition in your life that you've never questioned.

Now ask:

- Why do we do it this way?

- Who decided that?

- Is it good—or just old?

Then talk to someone about it. Be kind. Be curious. Be brave.

GR Explore the Word "Philosopher" — in Ancient Greek!

The word *philosopher* comes from two Greek words:

- philo (love)

- sophia (wisdom)

So a philosopher is... "one who loves wisdom."

Go to the Perseus Digital Library and search for these two words:

- φίλος (*philos*) — friend or love

- σοφία (*sophia*) — wisdom

What other English words come from these roots?

☐ AI Literacy Extension: Ask a Bot

Ask an AI:

"What makes someone a good leader?"

Then ask:

"Can someone love truth but be ignored?"

Compare its answers to what Socrates said. Do you agree more with the bot—or with the philosopher?

What's something *you* would return to the cave to say?

⬚ Dinner Table Conversations

1. Should tradition always be followed—or sometimes challenged?

2. What does it mean to "love wisdom" in everyday life?

3. Is it fair to expect someone to lead... even if they don't want to?

4. Would you leave comfort to help someone else see the truth?

5. Can a city (or a school... or a family) make space for quiet thinkers?

The Ship and the Storm

1: The Sea of Opinions

(Based on Republic 484a–487a – Why true philosophers are rare and mocked)

Scene:
 Socrates and the children stand near the harbor.
Boats rock in the wind. A group of men argue loudly by a market stall.

Milo (watching):
 Why do they all shout? No one's even listening.

Socrates:
 Because each one is sure he's right.
 But certainty is not the same as truth.

Tessa:
 Then what is truth?

Socrates:
 Let's ask this:
 Do you think most people love wisdom—or just love being right?

Milo:
 Being right. It feels better.

Socrates (nodding):
 That's why true philosophers are rare.
 They aren't satisfied with feeling right—they want to *be* right.
 And that takes time. Quiet. Courage.

Tessa:
So people ignore them?

Socrates:
Or mock them. Or fear them.
Because philosophers speak a different language.
They care more about truth than tribe, more about
reason than reward.

Milo:
So... real knowledge is lonely?

Socrates:
It can be. But it is also light in the darkness.

Under the Olive Tree

(The wind rustles the leaves. Tessa shields a candle
from the breeze.)

Tessa:
Socrates... why don't more people want truth?

Socrates:
Because truth doesn't flatter. It demands we change.

Milo:
So it's easier to live with opinion?

Socrates:
Yes. Like floating in a boat with no anchor.
It feels like freedom—until the storm comes.

Moral Conversation Prompt:

- Why do people argue without listening?

- What's the difference between "opinion" and "truth"?

- Is it better to feel right—or be right?

2: The Ship and the Captain

(Based on Republic 487e–489a – The parable of the ship of state)

Scene:
 Socrates leads the children along the rocky shore. In the harbor, a large ship is anchored. The sails flap loosely. Men argue on deck.

Socrates (pointing):
 Imagine a ship like this—but with no captain.

Tessa:
 Wouldn't it crash?

Socrates:
 Let's say the owner is asleep. The sailors start fighting over who gets to steer.

Milo:
 But none of them knows how to sail?

Socrates (nodding):
 Correct. They shout, trick, and even throw each other overboard.
 They say the true navigator is useless—because he doesn't flatter them.
 Because he studies the stars instead of politics.

Tessa (quietly):
 So they call the wisest one a fool?

Socrates:
 Yes. That is the tragedy of the city.
 The true philosopher knows how to steer—but no one trusts him.
 He is slow to speak, cautious to promise, and careful with truth.

Milo:
 But people want quick answers.

Socrates:
 And loud captains. But loudness does not lead a ship.

Tessa:
 So what does?

Socrates:
 Only the one who knows the stars—and loves the craft of steering.

Under the Olive Tree

(A driftwood stick lies in the sand. Socrates uses it to draw a ship and stars above.)

Milo:
Why does the true captain get ignored?

Socrates:
Because the others don't want a guide—they want a show.

Tessa:
So the best leader may be the one no one listens to?

Socrates:
At first, yes. But the storm reveals who knows the sea.

Moral Conversation Prompt:

- Have you seen people ignore someone quiet—but wise?

- What makes someone truly fit to lead?

- If the loudest person wants power, should we trust them?

3: Who Sees the Stars?

(Based on Republic 490a–497a – The training of the philosopher and the vision of truth)

Scene:
 Night falls. The children and Socrates climb a hill above the sea. The sky above is clear. Stars blink across the dark.

Socrates (pointing upward):
 Tell me—how does a captain steer at night?

Tessa:
 By watching the stars?

Socrates:
 Yes. But not every sailor can read them.
 Some see only dots. Others, patterns.
 But the true navigator learns the heavens—slowly, carefully, through years of study.

Milo:
 So the philosopher is like that? A star-reader?

Socrates:
 Exactly. A philosopher isn't born ready to rule.
 They must be trained—not just in facts, but in truth.

Tessa:
 How do you train for truth?

Socrates:
 First, learn to love what is. Not just what feels good.
 Then, seek what lasts—not just what changes.

Truth is not noise. It's not fame. It's not force.
It's something like the stars: constant, silent, deep.

Milo:
But what if someone doesn't care about the stars?

Socrates (smiling):
Then they may steer a boat—but never safely.

Under the Olive Tree

(The children lie back in the grass. Socrates traces constellations in the air with his finger.)

Tessa:
I used to think leaders needed confidence. Now I think they need patience.

Milo:
And quiet. The stars don't shout.

Socrates:
Yes. The soul trained for truth learns to see what others miss.
It waits, watches, and learns to rise above the fog.

Moral Conversation Prompt:

- What does it mean to be trained for truth?

- Can quiet thinking be stronger than loud opinion?

- Why might real wisdom be slow?

4: The Sun Beyond the Storm

(Based on Republic 507a–509c – The Sun as the symbol of the Good)

Scene:
Dawn. The children and Socrates are still on the hilltop. The sea is calm now. First light spills across the waves.

Socrates:
Now we come to the highest question.
Not just *how* we see... but *why* we see.

Tessa:
What do you mean?

Socrates:
The eye can see—but only if there's light.
And where does all light come from?

Milo:
The sun.

Socrates:
Exactly. Without the sun, you could have eyes... and still see nothing.

Truth is like that. Even the best soul needs something more. A light. A source. A reason.

Tessa:
So... truth comes from something else?

Socrates:
Yes. I call it the *Good*.
It is to the soul what the sun is to the eye.

Milo:
So "the Good" is like a sun in the sky of the mind?

Socrates:
Yes. It gives light to knowledge. Life to truth.
It is not a fact—but the reason facts matter.
It is not just a rule—but the reason rules work.

Tessa:
Can everyone see it?

Socrates:
Only if they climb beyond habit... beyond praise... beyond fear.
Most people live in shadow and think they see clearly.
Only the philosopher turns toward the light.

Under the Olive Tree

(The rising sun warms the olive leaves. The children squint, looking east.)

Milo:
 So all our learning... it's like walking toward the sun?

Socrates:
 Yes. Slowly. Sometimes painfully. But each step brings more light.

Tessa:
 And once you've seen it... you can't go back?

Socrates (softly):
 You can return to the shadows—but your soul won't be the same.

Moral Conversation Prompt:

- What does "the Good" mean to you?

- Why do we need light—to understand?

- What shadows might we mistake for truth?

📖 Conclusion: The Ship and the Storm

This chapter sailed into rough waters.

We saw why true philosophers are often ignored, why loud voices win the crowd, and why the soul that knows how to steer is the one people often fear most.

Socrates showed the children that being fit to rule isn't about power, passion, or praise. It's about patient training in truth.

The real leader is like a captain who studies the stars—even when no one is watching.

And beyond the storm, above the noise, there is a sun.

Not the one that warms the skin—but the one that lights the soul.

It's called the Good.

Most people never look for it. Some deny it exists. But the philosopher learns to turn toward it—and helps others climb.

Next, the children will enter the shadows themselves.

They will descend into the Cave.

☐ Final Section for Book VI

☐ Try It Yourself: Find the Signal

Today, everyone has opinions—online, in the news, at school.

Pick one question people argue about. Then:

- List 3 common *opinions* you hear.

- Then, look for someone asking a *better question*—not shouting, but seeking.

- Ask: who seems to want truth... and who wants to win?

Now try to be like the captain: quiet, steady, and guided by something higher.

GR Explore the Word "Good" — in Ancient Greek!

Plato uses the word ἀγαθόν (*agathon*) for "the Good."
It doesn't just mean "nice" or "not bad."
It means: *what gives life, meaning, and purpose.*

At the Perseus Digital Library:

- Search for: ἀγαθός (*agathos*)

- What other English words come from it? (Hint: Agatha, agathonics...)

What do *you* think is "good" in the deepest sense?

 AI Literacy Extension: Ask a Bot

Try this question:

"What does it mean to be good?"

Then ask:

"Can a machine be good—or only useful?"

Compare that to what Socrates said. Can the Good be programmed? Or only pursued?

⊡ Dinner Table Conversations

1. Have you ever seen someone wise—but ignored?

2. What's the difference between knowing facts and seeing truth?

3. Can you steer your life without looking at the stars?

4. What is "the Good" in your family? In your school? In your heart?

5. Would you trust someone quiet to lead?

The Cave and the Climb

1: The Cave

(Based on Republic 514a–517a – The allegory of the cave)

Scene:
 The children and Socrates gather near the opening of a cave. The early morning sun glows behind them. Socrates lights a torch and points into the darkness.

Socrates:
 Let me tell you a story.
 Imagine people born inside a cave. They've lived there forever—chained by their legs and necks.

They can't turn their heads. They see only a wall.
 Behind them burns a fire. Between the fire and the wall, other people walk by—holding up shapes and objects.

The chained ones see only the shadows. They think *that* is the world.

Tessa (shocked):
 They've never seen what's real?

Socrates:
 No. Only flickers. They give names to shadows. They believe they understand.
 But their eyes have never seen truth—only tricks of light.

Milo:
What happens if one escapes?

Socrates:
At first, he stumbles. The light blinds him. But
slowly, he begins to see:
The fire. The figures. The path.
And then... the way out.

He climbs. Each step is painful. But when he reaches
the surface—he sees the sun.

Tessa (quietly):
And then?

Socrates:
He goes back. Into the dark.

Milo:
Why would he do that?

Socrates:
To free the others. To tell them what he's seen.

But they laugh. Or get angry. They say he's broken.
They would rather believe the shadows.

Under the Olive Tree

(The children sit in silence. The cave looms behind
them. The sunlight touches the edge.)

Tessa:
That story feels real—even if it's not.

Milo:
It's like... I've seen shadows, too.

Socrates:
We all have. The cave is not a place—it's a habit. A fear. A comfort.

Tessa:
So climbing hurts?

Socrates:
At first. But staying in darkness hurts forever.

Moral Conversation Prompt:

- Have you ever mistaken something false for something real?

- Why might someone fight against truth?

- Would you return to the cave—to help someone else climb?

2: The Climb of the Soul

(Based on Republic 518b–521c – Education as turning the soul and the duty to return)

Scene:
The children walk with Socrates up a narrow path above the cave. The air is cooler now. Birds circle above.

Socrates:
What do you think is the soul's hardest task?

Milo:
Learning?

Tessa:
Changing?

Socrates:
Both. But the deepest task is this:
Turning.

Tessa:
Turning?

Socrates:
The soul must turn from what it knows—from shadows and comfort—toward truth.
That turning is the start of education. Not filling the mind with facts—but redirecting the whole heart toward the light.

Milo:
But what if someone doesn't want to turn?

Socrates:
Then they stay in darkness—even if they are smart.

The soul is not a bucket to fill. It is a living thing that must be aimed.

Tessa:
So education is aiming the soul?

Socrates:
Yes. Not by force. Not by shouting. But by guiding the eyes—gently, steadily—toward what is truly good.

Milo:
And once someone sees the truth?

Socrates:
They must return. Even if the others don't listen. The one who has seen the sun must go back into the cave—not for glory, but for duty.

Under the Olive Tree

(Socrates stops at a flat rock. The children sit down, the cave below, the sky above.)

Tessa:
So real learning isn't about answers—it's about direction?

Socrates:
Yes. The soul must *want* to rise—or it will not climb.

Milo:
And the one who climbs... must go back?

Socrates:
Always. That is the mark of the true philosopher—not escape, but return.

Moral Conversation Prompt:

- What helps you "turn" toward truth?

- Can someone be educated—but still live in shadows?

- Why must those who see clearly return to help others?

3: The Philosopher's Return

(Based on Republic 521c–525a – Why the philosopher must rule, and why they often do not)

Scene:
Evening settles on the hillside. The children walk back down with Socrates. Lights flicker in the cave below. A few people gather near the entrance, watching shapes on the wall.

Milo (whispering):
They don't know what's outside, do they?

Socrates:
No. And they may not want to. The shadows feel
safe. The sun feels strange.

Tessa:
But what if someone tells them? Shows them?

Socrates:
Many won't believe. They'll say the climb broke your
mind.
They'll say the sun is a lie. They may even grow
angry.

Milo:
So why go back?

Socrates:
Because the philosopher does not climb for pride.
They climb for truth—and return for love.

Tessa:
Even if it hurts?

Socrates:
Especially then.
The true philosopher leads not because they desire
to rule—but because they've seen what must be
done.

Milo:
But what if no one listens?

Socrates (gently):
Then the soul must still speak. Not to win—but to

witness.
Not to conquer—but to call.

Tessa:
So being wise means being brave?

Socrates:
Yes. And humble. And willing to walk both up—and back.

Under the Olive Tree

(The children look out over the city. A breeze stirs the leaves. Socrates sits quietly beside them.)

Tessa:
You've seen the sun, haven't you?

Socrates:
Enough to know where it rises. And enough to keep returning.

Milo:
Then maybe... we'll go back, too.

Socrates (smiling):
That is the work of the just soul.
To see—and to serve. To climb—and to care.

Moral Conversation Prompt:

- Would you return to help others, even if they didn't want help?

- What is harder: climbing toward truth—or walking back into confusion?

- Can real leadership come from love—not ambition?

📖 Conclusion: The Cave and the Climb

This is Plato's most famous idea—and maybe his hardest.
 The Cave.

Socrates showed the children what it means to live in shadows, to mistake noise for truth, and comfort for knowledge. He told them that education is not just learning—it's turning. Turning the soul away from illusion and toward the Good.

But the journey does not end with escape.

The one who climbs must return.

This is the mark of the philosopher—not pride, but service. Not escape, but witness.
 Even when mocked. Even when rejected.

This is also the challenge to us.
 Are we still watching shadows?

Or are we ready to turn, to climb, and to return—
bravely, patiently, lovingly?

☐ Final Section for Book VII

☐ Try It Yourself: Shadow Spotting

Pick one thing you believe is *definitely true.*

Now ask:

- Where did I learn this?

- Could it be a shadow?

- What would it feel like to let go of it—even for a moment?

Then try explaining it to someone else.
Ask *them* what they see. Maybe their eyes are looking at a different wall.

GR Explore the Word "Education" — in Ancient Greek!

Plato's word for education is παιδεία (*paideia*).
It doesn't mean just school. It means *the shaping of the whole soul.*

At the Perseus Digital Library, search for:

- παιδεία (*paideia*) – upbringing, formation, moral training

Can you list 3 things in your life that are shaping your soul?
 Are they turning you toward the light—or away from it?

AI Literacy Extension: Ask a Bot

Ask:

> "How can we tell if we're living in a 'cave'?"

Then follow up:

> "What are some modern 'shadows' people believe are real?"

Do the answers match what Socrates said?
 What "shadows" do *you* see today?

Dinner Table Conversations

1. Have you ever tried to help someone—but they didn't want help?

2. What's the bravest truth you've ever told?

3. Why do people resist change—even when it's good?

4. What makes someone wise—and why are the wise often ignored?

5. Would you return to the cave?

The Fall of the City

1: When Honor Replaces Wisdom

(Based on Republic 545c–550c – The fall from aristocracy to timocracy: when honor replaces reason)

Scene:
 The children and Socrates walk through the city square. The walls are still strong. The guardians still watch. But something feels... different.

Tessa:
 It looks like the same city. But it feels colder.

Socrates:
 That's because something invisible has changed.
 The rulers no longer seek truth. They seek *honor*.

Milo:
 Is that bad? Isn't honor good?

Socrates:
 It can be. But only when guided by wisdom.
 When honor takes the throne, reason steps down.

Tessa:
 What does that look like?

Socrates:
 People start to care more about reputation than reality.

They follow rules—but only to win medals.
They praise discipline—but only to be admired.

Milo:
So the city still looks strong—but it's weaker inside?

Socrates:
 Yes. The soul of the city begins to split.
 The spirit—remember the part that loves victory—
takes over.
 Desire is still held back. But reason? Pushed aside.

Tessa (frowning):
 That sounds like a soldier running the city instead of
a philosopher.

Socrates:
 Exactly. This is the city of *timocracy*—rule by honor.
 It obeys strength. It admires toughness.
 But it forgets the stars.

Under the Olive Tree

(The children sit near a stone pillar engraved with
names of fallen heroes. Socrates dusts moss from the
base.)

Tessa:
 So... wanting to be admired can break a city?

Socrates:
When honor matters more than truth, yes.

Milo:
But how do you tell the difference between real virtue—and just showing off?

Socrates:
Ask: would they still do it if no one were watching?

Moral Conversation Prompt:

- When is honor helpful—and when is it dangerous?

- Have you ever done something good… just to be seen?

- What happens when people care more about image than truth?

2: The Ambition of the Rich Man's Son

(Based on Republic 550c–555b – The fall from timocracy to oligarchy: when wealth becomes the ruler)

Scene:
The children walk through a newer part of the city. The buildings are taller. The streets are polished. Shops glitter with goods. A golden gate marks the entrance to a grand home.

Milo (peering in):
This city looks richer than ever.

Socrates:
Yes. But look closely. Who rules now?

Tessa:
Not philosophers. Not even warriors.

Socrates:
Now it is the wealthy.
This is the city of *oligarchy*—rule by the rich.

Milo:
But isn't wealth a sign of success?

Socrates:
Sometimes. But here, money becomes the measure
of worth.
The wise are ignored. The strong are hired. The poor
are forgotten.

Tessa:
So people aren't judged by virtue—but by coins?

Socrates:
Exactly. The city that once trained its soul... now
counts its silver.
The rulers care more about profit than justice.
They fear poverty—but forget truth.

Milo:
And what happens to the poor?

Socrates:
They are silenced. Separated. Sometimes starved.
And their children watch... and burn with envy.

Tessa (softly):
So even peace can hide injustice?

Socrates:
Yes. A quiet city can still be deeply divided.
And when wealth becomes king... something darker
waits nearby.

Under the Olive Tree

(A few coins sit near a merchant's stand. The
children watch a barefoot boy walk past with empty
hands.)

Tessa:
Socrates... is it wrong to want comfort?

Socrates:
Not at all. But when comfort matters more than
character, the soul shrinks.

Milo:
What happens when people are too afraid to lose
their stuff?

Socrates:
They guard gold instead of goodness. And the city's
heart grows cold.

Moral Conversation Prompt:

- Is money a good ruler—or just a useful servant?

- How can wealth hide injustice?

- What happens when the poor are silenced?

3: The Loud Voice of Freedom

(Based on Republic 555b–562a – The fall from oligarchy to democracy: when freedom overthrows order)

Scene:
 The children and Socrates enter a noisy plaza. Music plays from every corner. People shout, dance, argue, and sell. No one seems in charge.

Milo (wide-eyed):
 Everyone's doing whatever they want!

Tessa:
 Is this... freedom?

Socrates:
 Yes. And no.

This is the city of *democracy*—where freedom becomes the highest good.

Milo:
But isn't freedom good?

Socrates:
Like wine, it is good in measure—but dangerous in excess.

Tessa:
What does that mean?

Socrates:
In this city, every desire gets a vote.
People eat when they want, sleep when they want, believe what they want—even if it contradicts yesterday.

Milo:
So there are no rules?

Socrates:
There are laws—but they are bent by feeling.
The loudest voices get heard. The richest desires get served.
Order is mistaken for oppression. Guidance is called tyranny.

Tessa:
But people look happy.

Socrates:
At first. But when the soul obeys every craving, it forgets how to choose.

Milo:
So democracy begins with freedom... but ends in chaos?

Socrates (softly):
And in that chaos, something waits.
A voice. A promise. A tyrant.

Under the Olive Tree

(The children sit near a fountain. A banner flaps above them: "Let Everyone Be Their Own Master!")

Tessa:
I thought freedom meant choosing wisely.

Socrates:
It should. But here, freedom means never saying no—even to your worst impulse.

Milo:
So... when everyone tries to be king, no one rules the soul?

Socrates:
Yes. And the city begins to starve—not for food, but for truth.

Moral Conversation Prompt:

- When is freedom helpful—and when is it harmful?

- Can too many choices make it hard to choose well?

- What happens when no one wants to be guided?

4: The Birth of the Tyrant

(Based on Republic 562a–569c – The fall from democracy to tyranny: when desire becomes a master)

Scene:
 The plaza has grown tense. Crowds argue. Food is short. Everyone blames someone else. Then, a man stands on a platform—loud, charming, fierce.

Socrates (pointing):
 There. Do you see?

Tessa:
 Who is he?

Socrates:
 He is the tyrant. Born from democracy's freedom.

Milo:
 But people are cheering for him.

Socrates:
Yes. Because he promises everything. He says, "I will protect you." "I will punish the bad ones." "I will make things fair again."

But slowly, he takes more.
He removes his enemies. He silences the wise.
He rules not for justice—but for himself.

Tessa (nervous):
And people still follow him?

Socrates:
At first, they praise him. Later, they fear him.
And by the time they see clearly, it's too late.

Milo:
How does someone become like that?

Socrates:
It starts in the soul.

The tyrant's soul is ruled by *desire*. Not reason. Not honor.
His cravings grow louder than his conscience.

He cannot stop. He must have more.

Tessa:
So the tyrant is not just a ruler—but a broken soul?

Socrates:
Yes. A soul enslaved to its own appetite.
And when such a soul leads, the whole city suffers.

Under the Olive Tree

(The children sit under the olive branches. The cheers of the crowd echo behind them.)

Milo:
 He looked strong... but you say he's weak?

Socrates:
 He is strong in body. Loud in speech. But his soul is in chains.

Tessa:
 Chains made of... desire?

Socrates:
 Yes. The worst tyrant is not over others—but within yourself.

Moral Conversation Prompt:

- Can someone look powerful—but be ruled by desire?

- What makes a soul tyrannical?

- How do we guard our hearts—and our cities—against tyranny?

📖 Conclusion: The Fall of the City

Even the mightiest city can crumble when its soul forgets the path of truth. In This chapter we've seen how honor, wealth, freedom, and uncontrolled desire twist the order of a city and the spirit of its people. What once began in balance—a city built on need, nurtured by truth—has slowly decayed into divisions, greed, and finally, tyranny.

Socrates reminded the children:

> When honor replaces wisdom, the heart grows cold.
> When wealth dictates worth, justice is lost.
> When freedom is unmoored, chaos follows.
> And when desire commands without reason, a tyrant is born.

Yet even as the city falls apart, these changes are not the end. They serve as lessons—a call to look within and remember the values that once held the community together. The just city, like the just soul, can only flourish when every part works for the good of all.

May these reflections kindle a quiet strength in every young heart, showing that while cities may decay, the light of truth and wisdom can always be nurtured again.

🕮 Final Section for Book VIII

☐ Try It Yourself: The City's Mirror

Take a moment to think of a place you know—your school, neighborhood, or home. Consider:

- What parts of this place work well together?

- Which parts seem to pull away from each other or create conflict?

Ask yourself:

- How could things change if everyone cared more for truth than for personal gain?

- What small action might help restore balance?

Write or talk with a friend about what you see. How does the life of a city or community mirror the health of its people?

GR Explore the Word "Tyrant" — in Ancient Greek!

Plato uses the word τύραννος (*tyrannos*) to describe a ruler who seizes power through raw desire rather than wisdom.

- Visit the Perseus Digital Library to search for τύραννος.

- Can you think of modern words that sound alike? (Hint: "tyrant" is used in stories and everyday talk.)

Reflect on:

- What qualities make a leader wise?

- How can you spot when someone's desire for power overshadows their care for others?

 AI Literacy Extension: Ask a Bot

Try asking:

> "How does unchecked desire lead to injustice?"

Then follow up with:

> "What are ways to keep leaders in check today?"

Compare these answers with Socrates' lesson about the decay of order. Is truth protected when personal ambition reigns, or when shared values lead?

 Dinner Table Conversations

1. Have you ever seen a situation where someone's want for more hurt everyone?

2. What do you think is more important: personal gain or the good of the community?

3. Can you think of someone who uses wealth or popularity to control others?

4. Why is it sometimes harder to listen to reason than to loud opinions?

5. What small act could help bring balance back to a group or community?

The Tyrant's Heart

1: The Prison Inside the Palace

(Based on Republic 571a–576c – The tyrant's soul is the most enslaved and least happy)

Scene:
 The children and Socrates walk past a tall wall.
Inside, they glimpse the tyrant's palace—shining floors, golden plates, a dozen guards.

Milo (awed):
 He has everything. Why doesn't he look happy?

Socrates:
 Because what you see is a palace.
 What I see... is a prison.

Tessa:
 A prison?

Socrates:
 Yes. Not of stone or iron—but of *desire*.
 The tyrant's soul is full of cravings—loud, endless, competing.

He wants food. Power. Praise. Pleasure.
 He obeys them all—but none give him peace.

Milo:
So... he rules everyone—but not himself?

Socrates:
Exactly. His desires fight like wild dogs.
No voice of reason guides him. No friend tells him
no.

Tessa:
That sounds lonely.

Socrates:
It is. He trusts no one. He fears betrayal.
He must flatter some, crush others, and always
pretend he's strong.

Milo:
Even though he's weak inside?

Socrates:
The weakest of all.
The tyrant wears a crown—but his soul wears
chains.

Under the Olive Tree

(The children sit beneath the olive branches. In the
distance, a trumpet echoes from the palace.)

Tessa:
I thought having power would make you free.

Socrates:
True power begins with self-mastery.
But the tyrant's soul is mastered by its own
appetites.

Milo:
So desire isn't the enemy... but it can become one?

Socrates:
Yes. Desire should serve reason—not rule it.

Moral Conversation Prompt:

- Can someone have everything—and still feel empty?

- Have you ever felt ruled by a craving or habit?

- What makes someone truly free?

2: The Three Kinds of Pleasure

(Based on Republic 580d–583a – The hierarchy of pleasures: bodily, spirited, and rational)

Scene:
Socrates leads the children down a garden path. Three fountains bubble side by side: one with sweet-smelling water, one bright and bubbling, one still and clear.

Socrates (pointing):
Let's say each fountain gives pleasure. But not the same kind.

The first pleases the body—like food or sleep.
 The second pleases the heart—like honor, pride, or winning.
 The third pleases the mind—like understanding, wisdom, or truth.

Tessa:
 So which is best?

Socrates:
 Let's ask: which one lasts longest? Which one builds peace, not just excitement?

Milo (pointing to the clear one):
 That one feels... deeper.

Socrates:
 Yes. The first pleasure fades quickly.
 The second depends on others.
 But the third—rational joy—is quiet, lasting, and doesn't need applause.

Tessa:
 And the tyrant?

Socrates:
 He drinks only from the first—and gulps it fast.
 He never tastes the highest joy—because his soul never looks up.

Milo:
 So the just soul... drinks from the highest fountain?

Socrates:
 Yes. Slowly. Gratefully. And that joy fills the whole soul.

Under the Olive Tree

(The children sip cool water from a clay jar. Socrates watches them gently.)

Tessa:
 Why don't more people reach for the highest joy?

Socrates:
 Because it is quiet. It waits. It asks us to grow.

Milo:
 And the loud pleasures rush in first?

Socrates:
 Yes. But only the deepest joy makes the soul truly full.

Moral Conversation Prompt:

- Which kind of pleasure do you seek most often?

- Can quiet joys be stronger than loud ones?

- What does it mean to feed your soul—not just your senses?

3: The Just Soul Rejoices

(Based on Republic 581a–588a – The happiness of the just soul compared to the tyrant's misery)

Scene:
 Socrates and the children sit beneath a sprawling olive tree. The sun filters through the leaves, casting warm patches of light on the ground.

Socrates:
 Now, we have seen the tyrant's soul—chained and restless.
 But what of the just soul?

Tessa:
 Is it really happier?

Socrates:
 Yes. The just soul is like a calm sea—steady, deep, and full of life.
 It does not crave more than it needs. It finds joy in harmony.

Milo:
 Even if the just soul is poor or unknown?

Socrates:
 Especially then. True joy does not depend on gold or

fame.
It comes from within—when reason rules, and desire listens.

Tessa:
So the just soul is free?

Socrates:
Free as a bird that sings—not trapped by chains, but flying toward the sun.

Under the Olive Tree

(The children close their eyes and breathe deeply. A soft breeze stirs the branches.)

Milo:
I want a soul like that.

Socrates:
Then start today.
Choose what feeds your soul—not just what pleases your senses.
Listen to reason. Train your heart.

Moral Conversation Prompt:

- What makes someone truly happy?

- Can joy come from inside, not outside?

- How can you help your soul stay free?

🔲 Conclusion: The Tyrant's Heart

In This chapter, we have looked inside the soul of the tyrant and seen what true misery looks like. Though he rules over many, he is himself a prisoner—chained by desire, fear, and unrest. His pleasures are shallow, fleeting, and never enough. Meanwhile, the just soul—though humble, unknown, or poor—is freer and happier because it lives in harmony and truth.

Socrates reminds us that true power begins within. When reason leads, and desire listens, the soul sings. When desire rules, the soul is enslaved.

May this lesson guide every young heart toward freedom, wisdom, and joy.

🔲 Final Section

🔲 Try It Yourself: Soul Reflection

Think about a time you felt restless or unhappy—even if everything seemed fine.

- What desires were pulling you?

- Did your reason help you choose what truly mattered?

- What can you do to help your soul find peace?

Write or talk about your reflections.

GR Explore the Word "Desire" — in Ancient Greek!

The Greek word for desire is ἐπιθυμία (*epithymia*).
It can mean hunger, craving, or longing.
But it can also lead us away from reason.

At the Perseus Digital Library, search for ἐπιθυμία and see how it is used in ancient texts.

☐ AI Literacy Extension: Ask a Bot

Ask:

"How can desires help or hurt us?"

Then ask:

"What can make someone truly free?"

Compare these answers to Socrates' teachings about the tyrant and the just soul.

📖 Dinner Table Conversations

1. When have you felt ruled by a desire? How did you respond?

2. What does it mean to be free inside your own mind?

3. How can you help your friends or family find joy that lasts?

4. Why is it harder to listen to reason than to impulse?

5. What small choices can help your soul stay peaceful?

The Story That Must Be Told

1: Why Poetry Was Banned

(Based on Republic 595a–600a – Plato's critique of poetry and false stories)

Scene:
 The children and Socrates gather in a quiet garden.
Nearby, birds sing melodies. A scroll lies unrolled,
filled with verses and images.

Socrates:
 Long ago, some believed poetry was dangerous.
 Not all poetry—but the kind that tells lies.

Tessa:
 Lies?

Socrates:
 Yes. Stories that make gods seem foolish, heroes
weak, and wrong look right.

Milo:
 Why would people tell such stories?

Socrates:
 Because they entertain. They sound sweet. They stir
the heart.

Tessa:
 But if they're not true, don't they hurt us?

Socrates:
 Exactly. False stories poison the soul like bad food poisons the body.

Milo:
 So poetry can teach both good and bad?

Socrates:
 Yes. The city must guard its children's hearts from stories that make them less brave, less just.

Under the Olive Tree

(The children sit quietly. The scroll rests between them.)

Tessa:
 I like stories. But I don't want to be tricked.

Socrates:
 Neither do I. That's why we must choose stories carefully.
 True stories teach courage, truth, and beauty.

Milo:
 So stories are like medicine?

Socrates:
 Exactly. They can heal—or harm.

Moral Conversation Prompt:

- Have you ever heard a story that made you afraid or angry for no reason?

- What makes a story good for your heart?

- How can we choose stories that help us grow?

2: The Myth of Er

(Based on Republic 614a–621d – The story of the soldier who returned from death and saw the fate of souls)

Scene:
 Socrates and the children sit beneath the olive tree. The evening sky deepens into stars.

Socrates:
 Let me tell you a story—one that was told long ago by a soldier named Er.

Tessa:
 What happened to him?

Socrates:
 Er died in battle—but after many days, his body did not decay.
 His soul returned to life to tell what he saw beyond the world.

Milo:
What did he see?

Socrates:
He saw souls choosing their next lives.
Some chose wisely—others foolishly.

Tessa:
Why did it matter?

Socrates:
Because the soul's choices shape its journey.
The just soul chooses harmony, truth, and courage.
The unjust soul chooses desire, fear, and power.

Milo:
So life after death is a new beginning?

Socrates:
Yes. And what we do now guides that next step.

Under the Olive Tree

(The children look up at the stars, thoughtful and quiet.)

Tessa:
That sounds like a great responsibility.

Socrates:
It is. Every choice builds the soul's path.

Milo:
So being just isn't just good—it's wise?

Socrates:
Yes. Justice is not just for this life—but for all lives.

Moral Conversation Prompt:

- What choices shape who you become?

- How can thinking about the soul's journey change how you live?

- What does it mean to choose wisely?

3: The Soul's Final Choice

(Based on Republic 621e–629c – The final counsel on justice, the soul's journey, and living well)

Scene:
Socrates and the children sit in the fading light under the olive tree. A gentle breeze stirs the leaves as night slowly falls.

Socrates:
Now we come to the last question:
What should the soul choose?

Tessa:
Isn't justice the best choice?

Socrates:
Yes. Justice is the soul's true home.
It brings peace, strength, and joy.

Milo:
But what if justice seems hard? Or lonely?

Socrates:
The just soul is never truly alone.
It walks with truth and courage as companions.

Tessa:
What happens after we choose?

Socrates:
The soul moves onward—carrying its choices like seeds.
Good choices grow into joy and harmony.
Bad choices bring sorrow and chains.

Milo:
So living justly is like planting a garden?

Socrates:
Exactly. Every day is a chance to plant what will bloom.

Under the Olive Tree

(The children close their eyes and breathe deeply, feeling the calm night air.)

Tessa:
I want to plant good seeds.

Milo:
Me too.

Socrates:
Then you are on the path of the just soul.

Moral Conversation Prompt:

- What seeds do you want to plant in your soul?

- How can you choose justice each day?

- What helps you stay strong when it's hard?

📖 Conclusion: The Story That Must Be Told

In this final book of the Republic, we learned why stories matter—not just for fun, but for shaping who we are.
False stories can trap us in shadows. True stories can guide us to light.
Through the Myth of Er, we saw that the soul's journey doesn't end here—it continues, shaped by the choices we make now.

Justice is not just a rule but a way of living—a path that brings peace, strength, and joy to the soul.

Socrates invites us all to choose wisely—to plant good seeds that will bloom within us and beyond.

⬜ Final Section for Book X

⬜ Try It Yourself: Storytelling Reflection

Think about a story you love.

- What lessons does it teach?

- Does it make you feel brave, kind, or wise?

- Could you tell a story that helps others grow?

Try writing or telling a story that shares what you've learned about justice and truth.

GR Explore the Word "Mythos" — in Ancient Greek!

The Greek word for story or myth is μῦθος (*mythos*).
It means more than just a tale—it is a way of understanding the world.

At the Perseus Digital Library, search for μῦθος.
What other words come from this root? How do stories shape our thinking?

☐ AI Literacy Extension: Ask a Bot

Ask:

"Why do stories matter to people?"

Then ask:

"Can machines tell stories that teach justice?"

Compare answers to what Socrates says about poetry and myth. What do you think?

⊞ Dinner Table Conversations

1. What stories have helped you become who you are?

2. How can stories teach us to be brave and just?

3. Why is it important to choose stories carefully?

4. What choices will you plant as seeds in your life?

5. How can you help others tell better stories?

Thank you for journeying through *Plato's Garden: The Children of the Chair*.
 May the questions, stories, and truths you've explored grow with you—under your own olive tree.

www.ingramcontent.com/pod-product-compliance
Lightning Source LLC
Chambersburg PA
CBHW081643040426
42449CB00015B/3432